Nursery Rhymes

for Marketers

Laurissa J. Doonan

ISBN: 1974288552
ISBN-13: 978-1974288557

DEDICATION

This book is for all those marketers who face-palm daily, and to all those who catch themselves in the weeds, trying to stop the yelling, and remembering why we love marketing.

(To the person who bought my Unused Potential on eBay a few years back ... this part was not included in that auction.)

CONTENTS

Laurissa J. Doonan

WHY NURSERY RHYMES FOR MARKETERS?

Nursery rhymes remind us of a time in our lives when stories taught us basic lessons and helped us learn more conceptual ideas. Unlike the Victorian Cautionary Tales, nursery rhymes didn't scare us, they guided us in nurturing ways to listen, learn and absorb. They were our first exposure to content marketing, using stories to teach, without pressure. Sometimes we need to remember the basics, and smile as we do so.

MARY, MARY, MARKETING FAIRY

Mary, Mary, marketing fairy.

where do your click-throughs go?

To landing pages with targeted forms,

and content they want to know.

PETER, PETER, LEAD GEN FEEDER

Peter, Peter, lead gen feeder,

had a prospect but couldn't read her.

He put her in a funnel path,

And nurtured her like a sales empath.

HI, HI PROSPECT

Hi, hi prospect,

have you any needs?

Yes, sir, yes, sir,

I'm drowning in the weeds.

One team needs some copy,

another needs a brand,

and one wants for a mobile app

to reach across the land.

JACK FELT ILL

Jack felt ill & had quotas to fill,

and end of the month was nearing.

He set about a new campaign,

despite the sales team sneering.

Jack did research, then checked stats,

Took time to build out a plan.

He brought in the leads,

that fit their exact needs,

and heard the Sales Team cheering.

CMO COLE WAS

AN EXPERIENCED SOUL

CMO Cole was an experienced soul

and a marketing king was he.

He called for his team,

he called for ideas

and he called for a great strategy.

THERE WAS AN OLD CLIENT

There was an old client,

who lived in the past.

He lost so many sales,

feared business wouldn't last.

He called in the experts, a new agency,

then listened and followed,

and avoided bankruptcy.

Know Thy Customer

Deliver the **Right Message**,
at the **Right Time**,
on the **Right Platform**

EMPTY TEMPTING

Plain calls-to-action appeared on the search wall.

Plain calls-to-action caused budgets to fall.

Without targeted messages,

nor targeted times,

you couldn't save nickels and dimes.

MARKETING STRATEGY

The marketing strategist, wrote directions & plans,

to reach the client's goal.

~ ~ ~ ~ ~ ~

The creative designer, then took those plans,

to capture the essence of soul.

~ ~ ~ ~ ~ ~

The seasoned copywriter, worked off the concepts,

wrote words that made it all whole.

~ ~ ~ ~ ~ ~

The marketing strategist, got them all back

together,

and to the client presented the gold.

I'M A PRETTY PRINT PIECE

I'm a pretty print piece,

as you can surely see.

But without a message and a list,

I'm as useless as can be.

THREE MARKETERS IN TRANSITION

This isn't pure fiction,

three marketers in transition,

and how do you think they got there?

The writer, designer and strategy maker .....

they all ran away,

from a rotten condition.

'Twas enough to make competitors stare.

Will Market
for Food

HO HE HO HUM,

THE MARKETER NEEDS A VALIUM

Ho he ho hum,

I'm in desperate need of a valium.

CPC's are too high,

conversions too low.

Optimization & planning,

Simply wasn't done.

MARKETER, MARKETER,

ADD TO MY QUEUE

Marketer, marketer, add to my queue.

I need more leads to make it through.

My guys are idle,

my machines don't hum.

I must have sales or the news'll be glum.

THE FREELANCE WRITER

AND THE MUSE

The freelance writer,

pulled an all'nighter,

struggling to make a connection.

A new muse awoke,

and startled the bloke,

but inspired a whole new direction.

SING A SONG OF OUTCOMES

Sing a song of outcomes,

Of positive ROIs.

Newly minted dashboards,

for different level eyes.

When data was presented,

the numbers all made sense.

Now wasn't that the right approach,

to justify expense?

JACK'S STATS

Jack's stats had all gone flat,

his outcomes were verging on dire.

But a look at the numbers,

and not the percents,

showed his sales were actually on fire.

AS I WAS BUILDING UP MY BRAND

As I was building up my brand,

I met a group to lend a hand.

They had a team to deal with copy,

they said they'd stay away from choppy.

They had a team to deal with art,

they said they'd do it a la carte.

Copy, creative, digital plan,

I felt they sold me something canned.

HARK! HARK!

THE RESULTS ARE STARK

Hark! Hark!

The results are stark,

the client's misreading the news.

One says too low,

another says, "Oh no!"

and one's about popped a fuse.

MARY NEEDED

A MARKETING PLAN

Mary needed a marketing plan,

to help her business recovery.

But her agencies charged for basic audits,

calling them insights and discovery.

ITTY BITTY BUDGET

The itty bitty budget,

drove the agency away.

Closer creeped the deadline,

inching day by day.

Off popped the brain lock,

and out popped a new name.

And the freelancer agreed with it,

so success was soon reclaimed.

THE PLIGHT OF THE COPYWRITER

Now I sit me down to write,

with deadlines looming,

time is tight.

If sub-par copy should emerge,

I'll change it to my latest dirge.

ABOUT THE AUTHOR

Laurissa Doonan is an award winning marketer, having spent the past 30 years working in all facets for some of the largest brands, from Pfizer to Brother, Werther's to K'Nex. She's used her expertise to make companies money through effective communications, internal collaboration, and developing strategic marketing approaches. Whether it's B2B or B2C, technology or consumer brands, the core tenet of marketing always hold true, Know Thy Customer.

She has been a contributing author for lifestyle brands, corporate clients, and television shows, and continues to blog based on regular inspirations.

(and yes, she really did sell her Unused Potential on eBay. You can read about it here: https://goo.gl/vYKC8q

www.InsidesOut.life
www.Charter-Marketing.com